Little
Hawaiian
'Ohana
Cookbook

Little
Hawaiian
'Ohana
Cookbook

edited by Joleen Oshiro & Betty Shimabukuro
photography by Craig T. Kojima

MUTUAL PUBLISHING

This book is an abridgement of *Hawai'i's 'Ohana Cookbook: From Our Family
to Yours* (published in 2011).

ISBN: 978-1939487-22-3

   Library of Congress Control Number: 2013944384

All recipe photos © Craig T. Kojima Photography
Photography © Kaz Tanabe: pg. 25, 33, 38, 45, 61, 64, 77
Photography © Douglas Peebles: pg. 47 (cutting fish)
Photography from Dreamstime.com: pg. 11 © Yap Kee Chan, pg. 12
   © Glenn Price, pg. 13 © Lijuan Guo, pg. 22 © Yana Kabangu, pg. 30, 44
   © Du an Zidar, pg. 41 © Iwka, pg. 47 (parsley) © Johannes Gerhardus
   Swanepoel, pg. 52 © Riverlim, pg. 59 © Photomailbox, pg. 70 (wrinkled
   paper) © Zts, pg. 70 (coffee stains) © Mashe, pg. 72 © Andrzej Tokarski,
   pg. 80 © Nataliya Evmenenko
Photography from iStockPhoto.com: pg. 75 © Seung Jae Kim

First Printing, October 2013
Second Printing, October 2014

Mutual Publishing, LLC
1215 Center Street, Suite 210
Honolulu, Hawai'i 96816
Ph: 808-732-1709 / Fax: 808-734-4094
E-mail: info@mutualpublishing.com
www.mutualpublishing.com

Printed in China

Table of Contents

Introduction

The foods that populate family dinner tables and potluck buffets are infused with more than secret ingredients and refined techniques.

Whether we realize it or not, they're fortified with memories in the making, of people dear to us and the traditions we share.

Perhaps this is why food is such a big deal in the Islands. Family looms large in Hawai'i, but it's not enough to gather with loved ones. We must also feed one another. That sharing of sustenance becomes part of our fiber.

I am fortunate to have many family traditions tucked

away in my heart and mind. A dish of tofu salad, for instance, unleashes remembrances of New Year's Eve at Grandma Oshiro's house. With every bite of tofu, I can also recall Aunty Lois's chow mein, topped with shiitake, pork, carrots, water chestnuts, Chinese peas and lots of gravy. It shared space on the food table with Aunty Doris's baked ham, mac salad, and maki sushi, Aunty Margret's roast turkey with chestnut stuffing and Mom's lumpia and konbu maki. Not to

mention her tofu salad.

Most importantly, I remember the seemingly endless laughter and song. My dad and his siblings were a happy, musical bunch. Late into the night, they played 'ukulele and sang Hawaiian songs. At midnight, Aunty Helen would pop open the champagne as they sang "Auld Lang Syne" and hugged each other, a rarity in our Asian family.

The last of those parties took place about 15 years ago. Today just a couple of the siblings remain. How precious those memories have become. It just takes some tofu salad to recall them.

I'm hardly unique. Everyone has such remembrances.

It is with this understanding of the deep ties between food and family that we thank the folks who shared the recipes that make up this cookbook. We know that each one is imbued with the love, support and celebration that families come together to share.

— *Joleen Oshiro*

PŪPŪ

Lomi Salmon Spread

While attending a trade show at the Blaisdell years ago, some-one at a food booth handed me a toasted bagel sample with some spread on it. I inhaled the entire piece in one bite. It was so yummy. I had to recreate that recipe.

Whenever I share this spread at a gathering, everyone thinks I chop, cut, dice, and slice all day, but it's all done in one little tub of lomi salmon. Gently fold in the cream cheese and there you have it. It's a winner every time and very easy to make.

My nana taught me that if you use quality products, remark-able flavors will be discovered.

1 container Taro brand lomi salmon
2 blocks Philadelphia cream cheese

Soften cream cheese, drain lomi salmon, and mix well.

Serve on toasted bagels or low-salt crackers.

Submitted by the Haynes Family

Korean Chicken Wings

Serves 4

As a child, Korean chicken was one of my all time favorite foods. Golden fried chicken wings that were lightly dipped in a sweet and garlicky shoyu sauce. Whenever my mom would make them (and she made them often), we would devour every last piece! The empty platter was a sure sign that it was a family favorite. In addition, Korean chicken was one of the first dishes that I learned to cook successfully as a young teen!

2 pounds chicken wings
2 eggs, beaten
3/4 cup flour
3/4 cup cornstarch
oil for deep-frying

1 cup shoyu
3/4 cup sugar
1 tablespoon minced garlic
1 tablespoon sesame oil
2 tablespoons thinly sliced green onions
2 teaspoons toasted sesame seeds

Toss chicken in beaten eggs. Mix flour and cornstarch together and then dredge chicken one at a time in the flour and cornstarch mixture and shake off the excess. Deep-fry in batches in preheated oil until golden and cooked through. While frying the chicken, make the dipping sauce. Heat the shoyu, sugar, garlic, and sesame oil in a small pot on low until sugar dissolves. Remove sauce from heat and add green onions and sesame seeds. Dip the fried chicken in sauce before serving.

Submitted by Susan Yuen

I'a Lawalu
(Fish Steamed in Ti Leaves)
Makes 12 packets

My mom, "Aunty Mike," as everyone called her, was very popular. She was first on everyone's invite list. Her signature dish, I'a Lawalu, was always brought to the party.

Whenever butterfish would go on sale prior to the holidays, my mom would buy a couple of extra slabs. She would soak it in fresh, cold water, changing the water several times to remove most of the salt. Our job was to wrap the fish in ti leaves, creating a packet. It was a labor of love. The individually wrapped treasures were then gently placed in a steamer. Then, all we had to do was patiently wait. On New Year's Eve we would make about 150 packets.

At family gatherings, guests would quietly look to see if we brought lawalu. Before, when we asked, "What can I bring?" they would say, "Nuttin'." Now, they blatantly request lawalu!

2 pounds salted butterfish (substitute salmon, moi, or halibut)
3 ti leaves, washed and cut into 5-inch squares
6 Hawaiian chili peppers, sliced lengthwise
String

Soak fish in fresh cold water, changing water to rinse out the salt. Cut fish into 1-inch cubes.

Place cubed fish on ti leaf square with Hawaiian chili pepper cut side-down, making a package. Tie each package with string, securing with a knot. Place in a steamer and steam for 25 to 30 minutes.

For added flavor, include lu'au leaves, spinach, a slice of pork, bacon, or onion in each packet. Adjust the size of the ti leaves accordingly.

Submitted by Larry Shigaki

Scallion Pancakes
(Chung Yao Beng)
Makes 5 pancakes

My father-in-law Wah Chung Cheng is a master at wok cooking, measuring intuitively either by hand or rice cup. While living with my in-laws, every night there would be healthy delectable dishes along with family stories of leaving Guangdong Province in Southern 'China and opening a restaurant and raising four children in Hawaii.

He founded Kin Wah Restaurant in 1982 with his sister, Jane, and her husband, Kinsang Wong. They worked tirelessly, no holidays or weekends off. In 2000, he retired and is currently known as "Fired Dragon" on the badminton courts.

"Chung yao beng," a northern Chinese dish, was one of the first he taught me to make. He learned the recipe as an apprentice chef in Hong Kong and continued to prepare it for his family. In Hong Kong it is sold by street vendors, much like pretzels in New York City. It is a tasty marriage of fried crusty exterior and chewy inside layers akin to flat bread. It is simple to prepare and has tasty results appealing even to kids.

1-1/2 cups water
4 cups flour
Garlic salt, to taste
1/2 cup cilantro
1/2 cup green onions
Vegetable oil for frying

Mix the water and flour until a sticky dough forms. Flour your hands and a clean flat work area and knead the dough until the ingredients are fully incorporated. Cover and let the dough rest for 30 minutes.

continued on the next page

Flour your work area and rolling pin well. Keep a bowl of flour handy to keep your area floured well so the dough doesn't stick. Divide the dough into 4 to 5 equal pieces. Take one of the pieces and roll it into a pancake about 1/8-inch thick. Spread 1 to 2 tablespoons of oil on the dough and sprinkle generously with garlic salt, cilantro and green onion.

Start at one end of the pancake and roll it in one direction until you have a long cylinder. Roll the cylinder into a coil or snail shape. Squeeze to bind the folds and then roll it out flat again. Continue until you've prepared all the pancakes.

Heat 1 to 2 tablespoons of oil over medium-high heat. Fry the pancake on one side until browned. Flip and continue on the other side until done (approximately 3 to 4 minutes on each side). Remove the pancake to a cutting board. Using a paper towel, scrunch the finished Chung Yao Beng to separate the layers and add texture to the pancake. Add more seasoning if needed.

Cut into triangles or strips and serve plain or with a dipping sauce of shoyu, crushed garlic, chili oil, and more green onions.

The pancakes can be prepared a day ahead of time and stored in the refrigerator. Oil a plate well and place the pancakes on the plate. Separate each pancake with a piece of plastic wrap (also oil between each pancake and the plastic wrap). Make sure all edges of the pancakes are covered by the plastic, otherwise they will dry out and harden.

Submitted by Jamie Cheng

SALADS, SOUPS, STEWS, AND SIDES

Lūʻau Stew

Serves 8

This recipe came from my mom through our Hawaiian tūtū. My mom grew up in a small house way back in Pauoa Valley, on the corner of Booth Road. Back then, Pauoa Valley used a lot of the water resources that came from the surrounding mountains, so residents were able to maintain rice paddies and taro patches. Because of the large availability of taro leaves and the economical price of beef brisket, my tūtū was able to make a big pot of lūʻau stew for her very large family of ten. Then, when I was a child visiting tūtū on Sundays, tūtū would still make a big pot of lūʻau stew to kaukau. Brings back many fond memories of my tūtū and visiting her back in Pauoa Valley.

2 pounds lūʻau leaves
4 pounds beef brisket
2 tablespoons vegetable oil
2 cloves garlic
3 cans beef broth
5 cups water
1 tablespoon Hawaiian salt

Clean lūʻau leaves and save stems. Cut brisket into 2-inch pieces.

Heat oil in large, heavy pot and place in brisket with garlic cloves. Be sure garlic does not burn. When meat is brown, add broth, water, and salt. Simmer for 3 hours. Check liquid in the pot periodically. It should cover the beef. Add water as necessary.

When beef is tender add lūʻau leaves and simmer another 1-1/2 hours. Be sure that the leaves are well cooked. (A lot of shrinkage will occur with the leaves.) Serve with rice or poi.

Submitted by Ernie Bautista and Roxanne Tunoa

Aunty Marine's Meatless Pancit

Serves 4 to 6

A few years ago for Thanksgiving, my daughter, a vegetarian, asked me to prepare a meatless dish. I normally used ground pork as the base for my pancit, but I replaced it with dried shiitake mushrooms and it was just as tasty. Since then, I always prepare this dish for family gatherings. A memorable moment was when my niece, Renee, asked me to contribute this pancit for her child's birthday party. I brought 3 pans and zip—everything went.

1 small (1-ounce) package dried shiitake mushrooms, sliced
2 cloves garlic, minced
2 tablespoons cooking oil
2 cans chicken broth
1 bundle long rice
2 packages Canton pancit or wheat noodles (dried)
4 stalks green onion, chopped
1 small carrot, grated
Salt and pepper (optional)

Soak shiitake mushrooms in water. Drain. Soak long rice in warm water until soft. Drain and cut into 2-inch lengths.

Brown minced garlic in cooking oil. Add shiitake mushrooms and brown for about 2 minutes.

Add 2 cans chicken broth and bring to a boil. Add long rice and stir. Break up dried noodles, then add.

When liquid is absorbed, add green onions and carrot. Add salt and pepper, if using. Toss and serve. If not serving immediately, sprinkle a few tablespoons of chicken broth before serving to keep noodles from sticking.

Submitted by Marine Patao

Oxtail Soup

Serves 4

I'm Japanese, but I was married to a great Chinese cook. He learned to cook from his mother, and I learned to cook Chinese food from watching him, his mother, and his great aunt. Nothing was ever written down and you eventually learned to improvise. This final version of oxtail soup came after many good and bad attempts. I like vegetables in my soup so I added the daikon and carrots. It's a time-consuming process but worth it. I won an oxtail soup showdown at Punahou School. The judges said my version made them think of the oxtail soup they ate when they were growing up. I hope that my children will enjoy this soup for many years to come. Long, slow cooking is like life itself: a long, evolving process.

....

1 tray oxtail
2 tablespoons oil
2 inches fresh ginger, skinned and cut in half
1 can chicken broth and 1 can water
1 chung choi (salted turnip bundle, available in Asian food markets)
1 daikon, about 6 inches long, peeled and cut into half-moon shape
1 large carrot, peeled and cut in chunks
1 package (12 ounces) shiitake mushrooms, soaked and cut in half with stems removed
1 package blanched peanuts
Cilantro (optional), for garnish
Grated ginger, for dipping

Brown oxtails in oil in a large soup pot. Cover with water. Add ginger. Bring to a boil to clean tails, then drain and rinse.

Using the same pot, put in oxtails, ginger chunks, chicken broth, and water (add more water if necessary, to cover oxtails.) Add chung choi. Bring to a boil, then simmer until oxtails are tender to the touch.

Put liquid in a separate container and refrigerate oxtails and broth overnight. Fat will rise to the top and harden; scrape off hardened fat and discard.

Put 1/3 of the broth (it should look gelatinous) in pot with oxtails and heat on low.

Put the remaining broth and daikon, carrots and mushrooms in a separate pot and bring to a boil, then simmer until veggies are fork-tender.

Add peanuts after 30 minutes—watch your liquid levels. Combine both pots and taste broth to adjust water if it's too salty, then serve.

Submitted by Carol Chun

Maui Onion and Orange Salad

Serves 4

Mommy got this recipe from her godfather, Alfred Marteles, on Maui sometime in the mid-1980s. She thought this was a "haute" dish as it included "good expensive stuff": Dijon mustard. At that time, cooking was very "black and white," and combining two ingredients such as onions and oranges was unheard of. But it was so yummy and Uncle was overjoyed to share this dish with us. The only problem was that there were no measurements, so we had to go home and make it repeatedly until we could figure it all out. Yup, Listerine made a bunch of money off us in the next couple of months!

---

5 navel oranges, peeled
1 large Maui onion, thinly sliced and separated into rings
Zest of 1 lemon
3 tablespoons lemon juice
1 teaspoon Dijon mustard
1/4 cup olive oil
3 tablespoons orange juice
1/2 teaspoon salt
1/4 teaspoon pepper
1 bunch watercress, stems removed
1/3 cup minced fresh mint leaves (optional)

Peel oranges, removing all white membrane. Slice crosswise into round pieces, reserving as much as of the juice as possible. Place slices and juice in a serving bowl. Add onion rings and sprinkle with lemon zest.

In a separate bowl, whisk together lemon juice, mustard, olive oil, orange juice, salt and pepper. Pour over orange mixture, toss and refrigerate until serving.

To serve: Tuck watercress around edges of serving bowl and sprinkle with mint, if desired.

Submitted by Julie Robley

Simple Crock Pot Jook

Serves 4

I can remember always having to wait for Thanksgiving or some special event where turkey was served before my mom would make jook. Well, now I don't have to wait.

I love my crock pot! It's a trouble-free way to keep my family nourished and happy. We all have busy lives. It's a gift of balance to keep all the balls in the air at the same time.

I have a busy life working my day job then picking up Erin, my daughter, from school. Between soccer practice and piano, we barely have time to sit together for a family dinner, let alone shopping and preparing meals.

In the evening, after dinner, I fill my little crock pot with all the ingredients for the jook. The hard part—shopping for all the ingredients—is done earlier. Sun Chong Grocery has everything. All we do is call in our order, and when they see us pull into their drive way, they wheel out our groceries to our car!

Turn the crock pot on low for eight hours and wake up to the rich aroma of ham and rice gruel.

2 smoked ham hocks (see note)
5 quarts water
1-1/2 cups white rice
6 to 8 pieces dried mushrooms
1/2 cup raw peanuts
2 slivers ginger (optional)
Dried bean curd (optional)

Put ham hocks in the crock pot, fill with water, add rice, mushrooms, peanuts, ginger, and bean curd. Switch the crock pot on low for 8 hours. The crock pot can stay on for up to 10 hours. Can be started before you go to bed and you'll wake up to the aroma of fresh jook for breakfast.

Note: Smoked ham hocks can be substituted with smoked turkey or turkey bones.

Submitted by Steve Dung

Maui-Style
Hawaiian Stew

Serves 6 to 8

This was a popular family gathering dish of Ed Hirai, who passed away in 2011. He was born in Pā'ia, Maui, and was a longtime resident of Kula. Approximately one year before his passing, Ed said he learned this recipe from his mother, Miyuki Hirai of Pā'ia Store. This is a recipe appropriate for beginner cooks. In fact, Ed's famous words were "this soup is so easy to prepare." At his memorial service on February 14, 2011, 60 copies of Ed's handwritten recipes were distributed.

1-1/2 pounds stew meat
2 tablespoons oil
7 cloves garlic, minced
2 or 3 celery stalks, sliced
2 large carrots, sliced
4 large ripe tomatoes, chopped
Salt, to taste
2 Irish potatoes, sliced in chunks
1 sweet round onion, sliced
1 can tomato sauce
String beans or cabbage (optional)

In a big pot, fry stew meat in 2 tablespoons oil, until brown. Add water and boil for 20 to 30 minutes. Drain water and add new water, and boil again.

After water starts to boil, see if the water stays clean. If so, add garlic, celery, carrots, and chopped tomatoes. Let it boil for hours until stew becomes orange.

Add salt and potato chunks with sliced round onions and tomato sauce. Boil on low heat until done.

Submitted by Clarence Kawana

Portuguese Stew

Serves 8 to 10

This is a cherished dish from my mom, Adelaide Ramos Rapozo, who is 99 years old. She is the last living sibling of the Joseph Silva Ramos and Filesbertha Vasconcellos clan of 17 children who settled in the Pa'auilo Mauka-Pōhākea area of the Big Island in the early 1900s. In order to assemble this recipe, I had to literally measure each ingredient alongside my mom as she cooked. She cooked by taste. Early in my childhood, whenever Mom cooked this dish, the aroma of garlic and vinegar lingered throughout the house—not to mention out of the house and down the driveway. Even the neighbors knew what we were having for dinner.

5 pounds stew meat
3 cloves garlic, minced
1 small onion, diced
2 tablespoons raw sugar or 1-1/2 packets Splenda
1 or 2 small Hawaiian chili peppers
1-1/2 cups water
1 (6-ounce) can tomato paste
3/4 cup white vinegar
5 red potatoes, cubed
2-1/2 tablespoons rock salt
2 carrots, cut into 1-inch chunks

Brown stew meat with garlic and onion in large pot.
Add remaining ingredients. Cook over medium heat for 1-1/2 hours, adding additional water as needed, about 1 to 2 cups.

Submitted by Bernadette Rapozo-Mattos

Crozier Potato Salad

Serves 10 to 15

This recipe comes from my wonderful mother-in-law, Mary Kalei Crozier, who learned how to make it from her mother, Anne Wong Leong. The extra eggs in the salad enhance the taste. Mary, now deceased, made this dish on all occasions. When I made it for the first time, my husband grumbled that it didn't taste like his mother's. It became a heated topic between us. He kept saying that his mother used sweet onions, and I disagreed. It was vindication for me when I asked my mother-in-law, who said, "Oh, I just use whatever onion is on sale."

4 to 5 potatoes, boiled or steamed
18 large eggs, hardboiled and diced
1 large onion, diced
Salt and pepper, to taste
1 to 1-1/2 cups Best Foods mayonnaise

Mix all ingredients in the order listed. Chill overnight and serve the next day.

Submitted by Karen Crozier

MAIN
DISHES

Country Ribs

Serves 4

This rib recipe was given to me by Pam Baldwin, who I met while my husband and I were stationed in Korea. She told me she had the easiest pork rib recipe in the world—and she was right! You pour the sauce on a slab of ribs, put it in the oven and an hour and a half later you've got a great meal! The ribs were comfort food while we were living overseas, and I still make this recipe when I want something easy to make for dinner. Pam loved to cook for us and invited us over to eat her native Thai cooking (because her husband and son didn't like it!). I think of Pam and our time together in Korea whenever I make this dish.

1/3 cup water
1/3 cup shoyu
1/3 cup orange marmalade
1/3 cup ketchup
1 clove garlic, crushed
3 to 4 pounds pork ribs

Mix all ingredients and pour over ribs. Bake at 350°F for approximately 1-1/2 hours.

Submitted by Cynthia Rankin (Betty Min)

Pot Roast and Taro

Serves 6

This old recipe was brought from Germany by my great-grandparents. The original recipe had potatoes, but I adapted it and added taro. We include this dish at every occasion and every get-together to celebrate them.

1 (5-pound) chuck roast (well-marbled)
10 carrots, peeled and sliced
2 large white onions, chopped
Water
Red wine (Burgundy or whatever you have)
1 box beef broth
Bay leaves
2 tablespoons cornstarch
Salt, pepper, herbs (your choice of herbs: rosemary, sage, thyme), to taste
3 large taro, peeled and cubed

This pot roast must be cooked in a pressure cooker for about 1 hour or in a heavy casserole pot in the oven for 1 to 2 hours at 350°F.

Brown pot roast on all sides in butter. Put everything in the pot with equal parts water, wine, and broth to cover the meat. Add a few bay leaves. Cover and cook for about 1 hour, until meat is tender when pierced with a fork.

Remove meat, onions, and carrots to serving platter. Cover with foil to keep warm. Mix 2 tablespoons cornstarch with a tiny bit of water just to moisten. Using a whisk to stir the gravy, add the cornstarch slowly a bit at a time while gravy is simmering. The gravy should start to thicken. Add more

continued on the next page

cornstarch and water if necessary. You must stir constantly to prevent lumps. Add any herbs you like and salt and pepper. Transfer the gravy to a bowl for serving.

Taro:

Use regular Hawaiian taro, Lehua, or something similar. Peel and cut up in uniform pieces. Boil in water for about an hour, covered, for large taro pieces and check until fork-tender. Serve with the gravy and meat. Leftovers can be cut up and fried with cut up bacon and onions for breakfast with fried eggs.

Submitted by Annetta Kinnicutt

Pork and Green Beans

Serves 8

I learned this recipe from my mother, who had been preparing it for us since I was a kid. My mom is now 90 years old and she no longer cooks. She said it's a very simple dish that she used to prepare every now and then. Whenever green beans were unavailable, she would substitute any vegetable in season.

3 pounds pork chops
1 clove garlic, minced
1 medium round onion, sliced
1 large tomato, sliced
1/4 cup shoyu
1-1/2 cups hot water
Salt and pepper, to taste
3 pounds fresh green beans (snip ends and French cut)

Cut pork chops into bite-size slices. Brown pork chops in a roomy pot or large, deep skillet. Add garlic, onion, tomato, shoyu, hot water and mix well. Bring to a boil. Simmer for 30 to 45 minutes until pork is tender. Taste and add salt and pepper if needed. When pork is done, add green beans and mix. Bring to a boil, cover and cook until desired tenderness of green beans.

Submitted by Lenora Ponce

Local-Style Barbeque Spareribs/Chicken

Serves 6

My husband, Hayden's, mom, Irene Punohu, always prepared delicious Chinese-style spareribs for our family dinners at her home in Kalihi. She was a good role model and a self-taught cook. Dinners were extra special when our children, Rachel and Trevor, anticipated her spareribs that were made with her special touch. She was proud of her dish and willingly shared her recipe.

I love to cook. On one occasion, I found this spareribs recipe. I modified the recipe to include a few more ingredients and made it for a get-together. My mother-in-law enjoyed it, praised my efforts and even asked me for the recipe! This recipe has been a loving reminder of all the special memories and fun we have shared together.

5 pounds BBQ ribs or 5 pounds chicken pieces
Large piece ginger
3 to 4 cloves garlic
Green onions

Sauce:
1 cup white sugar
1 cup ketchup
3/4 cup shoyu
1/4 cup oyster sauce

Boil ribs with ginger and garlic until tender. Combine sauce ingredients and pour over ribs or chicken. Broil ribs with sauce until golden brown. If using chicken, bake at 350°F for 45 minutes.

Submitted by Lorna K. Hu

Foo Chuck with Squid

Serves 4 to 6

This recipe has been passed down from my husband Robert's uncle, Aeko Jones.

(6-ounce) package foo chuck (dried beancurd sticks), Two Swallow brand
2 ounces black fungus (chien gee or wood ear)
2 tablespoons oil
1 thumb fresh ginger, smashed
2 cloves garlic, minced
1 pound pork, thinly sliced
1 pound fresh squid, boiled and cut into bite-size pieces
3 tablespoons oyster sauce
1 (14-ounce) can chicken broth
8 medium-sized dried shiitake mushrooms, soaked, rinsed and sliced
2 tablespoons cornstarch (mixed with a little water for thickening)
1/4 pound snow peas

Soak foo chuck in cold water until softened, at least 2 to 3 hours. Drain water and cut into 1-1/2-inch pieces. Soak fungus in cold water for about 45 minutes. Rinse several times and be sure to pick off any wood bits.

Heat pan or wok and add oil, ginger, garlic, and pork. Stir-fry for 3 to 4 minutes. Add squid, oyster sauce, and chicken broth and simmer for 5 minutes until pork is tender. Add foo chuck, black fungus, and mushrooms. When sauce comes to a boil again, add cornstarch slurry and snow peas. Stir until slightly thickened. Remove from heat, ready to serve.

Submitted by Jody Domingo

Napua's Slow-Cooked Kālua Pig with Rosemary and Maui Onions

Serves 6 to 8

I've been working on this recipe for years ever since I discovered that the crock pot works just as well as the oven for making kālua pig. I have family in Michigan who use this recipe at least once a month. It's a big hit at the church potluck! The secret is in the liquid smoke and 'alae. I add some of the cooking liquid to the meat just before serving to keep it moist. The rosemary and Maui onions give the pork a little extra flavor that you don't normally find in your traditional kālua pig.

5 pounds bone-in pork butt
1/4 cup liquid smoke
1/2 cup water
1 tablespoon dried rosemary
1/2 teaspoon black pepper
2 tablespoons 'alae salt (red sea salt)
1 small Maui onion, thinly sliced
1 small head cabbage, steamed and shredded
Additional 'alae salt, to taste
Steamed white rice

Place pork fat-side up in a 6-quart crock pot. Combine liquid smoke and water; pour over pork. Sprinkle with rosemary, black pepper and 2 tablespoons 'alae salt. Place onion slices around pork. Cover and cook on low for 6 to 8 hours, or until the pork is very tender. Transfer pork and onions to a large pan or bowl. Discard the fat and bone and reserve 1/2 cup of the liquid. Using 2 forks, shred meat into small pieces or chunks. Add shredded cabbage. Pour reserved cooking liquid over meat and sprinkle with additional 'alae to taste. Serve over rice and enjoy!

Submitted by Elizabeth "Napua" Poire

Mom's Mahimahi Sauté Belle Meuniere

Serves 4

My mom used to prepare this as a special meal on the weekends because during the week, she worked at my uncle's store in Pu'ukoli, and by the time she returned home, she couldn't prepare this dish in time for dinner. Because we had four children in our family, she had to prepare another entrée for my dad and two brothers, and we would enjoy a nice family meal together on Saturdays or Sundays.

Because the mahimahi was thick, I remember her slicing them on a slant to make thinner pieces.

8 (3-ounce) pieces mahimahi, thawed if frozen
1/4 cup milk
1/2 cup flour
1/2 teaspoon paprika
1 teaspoon salt
1/4 teaspoon ground white pepper
1/4 cup vegetable oil
1 teaspoon chopped parsley

Sauce:
1/2 to 3/4 stick butter
1 to 2 cloves garlic, minced
Juice from 1/2 lemon

Lemon slices (garnish)

Remove skin from fish. Cut into pieces by slicing on a slant to create thinner slices. Place in bowl with milk. Combine flour, paprika, salt and pepper. Remove fish from milk and dredge in flour mixture.

Heat oil in skillet; brown fish fillets and place on serving platter. Sprinkle with more paprika and parsley.

To make sauce: Melt butter in skillet. Add garlic. Add lemon juice. Cook until garlic is lightly browned. Pour sauce over fish; garnish with lemons slices.

Submitted by Lolly Saari

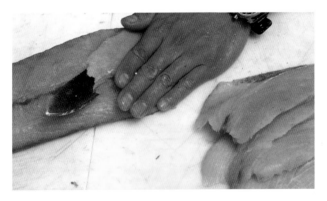

Seafood Curry

Serves 12

In my family there's no better way to bring generations together than over a steaming bowl of seafood curry. Not traditional "comfort food," it's still a mixture of ingredients that works well together to create a tasty fine dish similar to my family growing up of five adopted kids from around the world—eldest two from Quebec, middle child from Italy, and youngest two from Chicago. When I was ten, we moved to Pupukea where, while growing up, the many interesting and delicious foods cooked, shared, or tasted made me want to learn how to cook.

My mid-Westerner mother, Virginia Schergen, never strayed too far from the foods that she knew leaving me on my own. At the library the local cookbooks helped me develop versatility in the kitchen.

This recipe actually evolved from one on the side of a Kingsford Baking Powder box. As I got more daring, I started using coconut milk and different combinations of seafood. My seafood curry has been able to cross the cultural borders of my own diversified ethnically growing family. Originally not everyone was fond of curry but the dish grew to be a must for special occasions. Pleasing my family makes this an even more special dish.

Sauce:
6 tablespoons yellow curry powder
6 tablespoons flour
6 tablespoons butter
1-1/2 cups milk
1-1/2 cups canned coconut milk
Salt, to taste

1/2 cup diced onion
1 tablespoon butter

continued on the next page

49

Garlic salt, to taste
1/2 pound large scallops, connective tissue removed, cut in
    quarters
1 pound shrimp, peeled and deveined
1 piece sashimi-grade block 'ahi (or other fish, as desired),
    sliced 1/4-inch thick
8 ounces imitation crab pieces, cut in quarters
8 ounces frozen peas

To make sauce: Combine curry powder and flour. Melt butter
in saucepan. Add curry and flour mixture, stirring 1 minute,
until well mixed. Slowly whisk in both regular milk and coconut milk. Add salt and stir until sauce is boiling and thickened. Remove from heat. Cover with plastic wrap—let the
plastic touch the surface, to keep a skin from forming.

Rinse seafood and dry on paper towel.

In a large skillet or dutch oven, sauté onions in butter. Add
garlic salt. Once onions are translucent, add scallops, shrimp,
and fish. Sauté, stirring occasionally until shrimp are pink
and scallops are done. Add curry sauce, stirring gently.

Cut crab "legs" into quarters. Cook frozen peas as directed
on bag. Add both to curry. Taste before serving and add more
salt or garlic salt if needed. Simmer 5 minutes.

Serve with hot rice. May be garnished with mango chutney,
fresh shredded coconut, and raisins.

Submitted by Joanne V. Schergen

'Ōpakapaka
with Chinese Cabbage

Serves 2 to 4

Out of all the recipes my mother passed on to me over the years, this dish is my favorite. Not only is it really delicious, it tastes and looks like it was prepared by a chef from a Chinese restaurant. My mother encouraged me to cook, and this was my first successful fish dish that everyone loved.

'Ōpakapaka or mullet, cleaned
Salt and pepper to season
Flour for dredging
Oil for frying fish
1 stalk green onion, chopped

Gravy with Vegetables:
2 tablespoons chung choi (Chinese salted turnip),
   rinsed and chopped
4 shiitake mushrooms, soaked and sliced
1 small head Chinese cabbage, cut in 1-1/4 inch slices
1 piece garlic, crushed
1 piece ginger, crushed
1 teaspoon salt
1 teaspoon shoyu
1 teaspoon sugar
1-1/4 cups water
2 tablespoons cornstarch mixed with equal amount water

continued on the next page

Sprinkle salt and pepper on fish. Coat with flour. Heat about 3 tablespoons oil and fry fish on medium heat. When fish is cooked, place onto serving platter and immediately sprinkle green onion over fish. In same frying pan used to cook fish, fry chung choi and mushrooms. Add Chinese cabbage and stir fry. When almost done, add garlic, ginger, seasonings, and water.

Thicken with cornstarch mixture. Pour Chinese cabbage and gravy over fried fish. Serve hot.

Submitted by Jean Watanabe Hee

Chinese Sweet and Sour Spare Ribs

Serves 6

My mother, Popo Len, was the master chef of the Len clan. She arrived from Canton, China, in the 1930s and spoke all dialects. Everyone went to her for advice.

My family owned Lenwai Store in Lahaina. Then, in 1948, we moved to Makiki on O'ahu and opened Punahou Market, the current site of PeeWee Drive Inn. Popo Len would cook lunch daily. She cooked ginger chicken soup, squash soup, lilyroot soup, and beef stew. The smells from Popo's cooking were intoxicating. Neighborhood businesses asked if she could sell lunch to them, too.

Asking Popo Len for a recipe was like asking for a beating. It was "a little bit of this, a pinch of that, or about that much." You had to just watch multiple times to see how much to add or what to do. This made it very difficult to learn and get it just right. I guess all great cooks are like this. Every time you asked a question, you got scolded, "I told you how many times!"

My wife was surprised to find this recipe in Popo's recipe box with measurements. Everyone who eats this raves about it. It's simply delicious and easy to make. I always give the credit to my wonderful mom. Thank you, Popo.

---

3 pounds spare ribs (usually found in slabs)
1/4 cup vegetable oil
2 slices ginger
2 cloves garlic, crushed
3/4 cup Japanese rice vinegar
3/4 cup brown sugar, firmly packed
1/2 cup water

Marinade:
2 tablespoons shoyu
3 tablespoons cornstarch
1-1/4 teaspoons salt
1 tablespoon sherry

Pineapple chunks (garnish)
Cilantro (garnish)

Wash ribs and remove gristle. Pat dry with paper towels.

Combine marinade ingredients and pour over ribs. Let soak 10 minutes.

Heat oil in saucepan. Add ginger and garlic. Add ribs and brown. Drain fat. Add vinegar, brown sugar, and water. Simmer 30 minutes.

Note: Ribs may be served with pineapple chunks and/or garnished with cilantro.

Submitted by Norman Len

DESSERTS

Pineapple Cream Cheese Pie

Makes 1 (9-inch) pie

Grandma, Juanita Pagan Catania, married young and was a happy homemaker. She smiled all the time. My sister, Ro, and I loved her famous pineapple cream cheese pie. It was the highlight of every special occasion. Once in a while, for no reason at all, she would surprise everyone with this special treat. Eventually my grandparents moved from Hawai'i to California. The tradition continued—whether they came home to visit or we went to them, pineapple cream cheese pie was on the menu.

Now my twin daughters, Sammie and Sydney, help in the kitchen baking chocolate chip cookies, brownies, and of course, Gram's favorite dessert. It's memories in the baking. Now we share this little piece of heaven with you.

Pineapple filling:
1/3 cup sugar
1 can (9 ounces) crushed pineapple (do not drain)
1 tablespoon cornstarch
1 (9-inch) pie shell, unbaked

Cream cheese mixture:
8 ounces cream cheese, softened
1/2 cup sugar
1/2 teaspoon salt
4 eggs
1/2 cup milk
1/2 teaspoon vanilla

Preheat oven to 400°F. For the pineapple filling, combine all the ingredients and cook on low heat, stirring constantly until thick and clear. Let cool completely then evenly spread into pie shell.

To make the cream cheese mixture, blend cream cheese with sugar and salt. Add in eggs. Add milk and vanilla and mix thoroughly.

Pour over pineapple layer. Bake for 10 minutes then lower temperature to 325°F and bake for another 45 minutes.

Submitted by Janell Europa

Mango Bars

Makes 4 dozen bars

This recipe started out as an apple bar recipe, but my love for our local produce—especially Island mangoes—gave me the idea to replace the apples with mangoes. You can substitute the mangoes with other fruits as well, including peaches, prunes, apricots, etc. This recipe is special to our family because it's a delicious and somewhat healthier snack than store-bought fruit or cereal bars.

Crust:
2 cups flour
1/2 cup sugar
1 cup butter

Filling:
4 cups chopped mango
3/4 cup sugar
1/3 cup water
1 teaspoon lemon juice
3 tablespoons cornstarch, dissolved in 3 tablespoons water

Topping:
2 cups quick oats
1/4 cup flour
1/2 cup sugar
2/3 cup butter

Preheat oven to 350°F. To make crust, combine flour and sugar in a bowl. Cut in butter. Press into 9x13-inch pan. Bake 7 to 10 minutes, until lightly browned.

For filling, combine mangoes, sugar, water, and lemon juice in a pan. Cook about 10 minutes, until mangoes are tender. Stir in cornstarch slurry and cook until thickened. Cool slightly. Pour over prepared crust.

To make topping, combine oats, flour, and sugar. Cut in butter. Sprinkle over mango mixture. Bake 50 minutes. Cool and cut into bars.

Submitted by Lillian Kashiwabara

Panipopo
(Samoan Coconut Rolls)
Serves 8 to 10

Panipopos are a sweet treat. Whenever my husband, Eddie, is homesick for Samoa, he asks me to make these coconut rolls. They are a favorite dessert of our kids, nieces, and nephews. Whenever our relatives are in town or over for dinner, they request panipopos for dessert.

1 cup evaporated milk, very warm
1 tablespoon yeast
1 tablespoon sugar
1/4 cup sugar
3 eggs
1 teaspoon salt
3-1/2 cups flour, plus 1 more cup as needed
1/2 cup melted butter

Coconut Sauce:
2 cans coconut milk
3/4 to 1 cup sugar
3 tablespoons cornstarch dissolved in 1/4 cup water

Combine milk with yeast and 1 tablespoon sugar. Let sit until foamy.

Mix together: 1/4 cup sugar, eggs, salt, flour, and butter. Add yeast mixture; knead until smooth. Add up to 1 cup more flour as needed, just enough to make dough smooth and elastic. Let rise one hour; punch down. Let rise another 30 minutes. Shape into rolls and place in large pan. Let rise while you make the coconut sauce.

To make sauce: Combine coconut milk and sugar in saucepan and heat, stirring to dissolve sugar. Add cornstarch mixture, stirring constantly, until it begins to thicken. Pour over rolls. Let sit 15 minutes.

Preheat oven to 375°F. Bake rolls 20 to 25 minutes, until golden brown.

Submitted by Jenni and Eddie Maiava

Buko Salad
(Filipino Ambrosia Fruit Salad)
Serves 6 to 8

It's been about 25 years since I first stumbled upon this recipe for ambrosia salad with a twist. When I started taking it to gatherings, it was a hit and continues to be a favorite. This dessert is addicting, and it seems everyone just can't get enough of it so I make a lot. "Buko" means coconut in Filipino.

1 large can fruit cocktail or tropical salad chunks (available at Sam's Club)
1 bottle kaong (palm nut in heavy syrup)
1 bottle coconut or pineapple gel (in syrup)
1 bottle macapuno strings (coconut strings in heavy syrup)
2 pints whipping cream

Drain fruit well. Rinse and drain kaong, coconut or pineapple gel, and coconut strings (separate strings).

Mix all ingredients in a large container. Chill well and serve.

Submitted by Susan M. Segawa

Walnut Cupcakes

Makes 24 cupcakes

In the '70s I was living in 'O'ōkala on the Big Island with my mom, Granny, my husband, Glenn, and our children, Jan and Lee. Granny was always into buying gadgets. One day out pops this brand new Vitamix mixer with a shiny stainless steel bowl. Well, I tested it with this bundt cake recipe that I got from a friend at school. I began to measure each ingredient from the top of the page, working my way down. At the end of the ingredient list I read the instructions, and yikes, the walnuts, cinnamon, and sugar were for the topping! I had mixed them all up! All I could do was push the start button on the mixer. I baked it and my "mistake" walnut cake was a big hit with my family. I usually use a 7x11 cake pan to get the cake taller.

....

3/4 cup water
3/4 cup popcorn oil
1 teaspoon vanilla
4 extra large eggs
1 box (18.25 ounces) Duncan Hines butter cake mix
1 (5.1-ounce) box JELL-O vanilla instant pudding
1 teaspoon cinnamon
1 cup chopped walnuts
1 (13.5 ounce) Easy Frost Cream Cheese Frosting, for decorating

Preheat oven to 350°F. Mix water, oil, vanilla, and eggs. Add remaining ingredients. Mix on medium speed 2 minutes. Pour batter into 24 cupcake liners in muffin pan. Bake for 20 minutes. Insert a toothpick in the middle of one of the cupcakes. If it comes out clean, the cupcakes are done.

Note: If you would like to make a cake instead of cupcakes, a 7 x 11-inch cake pan can be used. Bake for 45 to 50 minutes.

Submitted by Fern Yamane

Mom's Homemade Liliko'i Jelly

Makes 12 (4- to-6-ounce) jars

My mom, Mildred Tam Chun, is remembered for her original treats and liliko'i jelly. From her own liliko'i vine, Mom harvested more than 100 fruit to prepare yummy treats. I remember picking liliko'i as a child in our Mānoa yard. Scooping the fresh pulp and straining the juice was a time for bonding with mom. Sweet liliko'i fragrance was everywhere, and we made liliko'i jelly, candies, pies, cakes, frostings, and more. Everyone loved receiving jelly at Christmas because it was home grown, straight from the vine and made with lots of love.

6-1/2 cups sugar
1-1/2 cups water
1 (6-ounce) bottle Certo pectin
1-1/2 cups fresh liliko'i concentrate
1 (8-ounce) block paraffin wax

Place sugar and water in a large saucepan and mix well. On high heat, bring to a rolling boil and cook for 1 minute, stirring constantly.

Remove from heat and immediately stir in Certo. Add liliko'i juice and mix well. Pour quickly into sterilized jars. Cover at once with 1/8-inch hot paraffin. Refrigerate jelly.

Submitted by Yvonne Chun Izumi

REMEMBERING

The Willows Curry

In the 1940s, Emma Hausten and her family dreamed of offering the finest in gracious hospitality that would mimic the relaxing atmosphere of home ... the kind of place reserved for friends and family to gather and share the important moments of the day. On July 4, 1944, the Hausten 'ohana realized their dream by opening The Willows, a restaurant where everyone was welcomed with aloha.

Today, a visit to The Willows is a step back to a time when guests were greeted by the melodious sound of Hawaiian music, the fragrance of plumeria, and a sweet komomai—welcome. Here is where curry, mango chutney, and coconut sky high pie became famous.

Curry Sauce:
3 garlic cloves, minced
1/4 cup fresh chopped ginger
2 cups finely chopped onions
6 tablespoons clarified butter
3 teaspoons salt
3 teaspoons sugar
3 tablespoons curry powder
9 tablespoons flour
8 cups coconut milk

2 pounds boneless chicken thighs, cut into bite-sized pieces
6 ounces white wine or dry vermouth
3 tablespoons peanut oil
Salt and pepper to taste
6 tablespoons curry powder

continued on the next page

Sauté garlic, ginger, and onion in clarified butter. Add salt, sugar, curry powder, and flour. Mix thoroughly. Add coconut milk a little at a time, stirring to a smooth thickness, and cook for 20 minutes until sauce begins to boil. Allow to stand several hours. Strain before using.

Marinate chicken in white wine or dry vermouth and peanut oil. Add pinch of salt and pepper. Let stand 15 minutes. Pan fry curry powder in saucepan. Add marinated chicken. When chicken is cooked, pour in curry sauce.

Note: Pictured is The Willows Curry with chicken which can be substituted for shrimp.

Submitted by Ray Orozco who worked at The (Original) Willows

New Year's Day Korean Man Doo

Serves 4 to 6

My Korean grandmother, my father's mother, used to make this man doo dish at our annual New Year's feast with other incredible Korean favorites like bulgogi, kalbi, and fish jun. All types of kim chee and various side dishes were served, including warabi, or fern shoots Korean-style, and soybean sprouts that were individually cleaned by taking the root off the end and made into namul (salad). There were a lot of New Year's traditions, and this dish was significant and eaten with the family during the holidays.

I enjoy keeping the tradition alive now that my grandmother is no longer with us, and I look forward to making my rendition of this incredible Korean dinner on New Year's Day. Grandma Ro usually prepped for a few days. We would arrive at her home in Wahiawā and help her make the man doo. I remember her adding different ingredients back then, but I've altered her recipe according to my personal taste.

---

2 cups kim chee cabbage, chopped and drained

2 cups firm tofu, chopped and drained

2 cups bean sprouts, blanched and chopped

1 pound ground pork (ground turkey can be substituted)

2 tablespoons sesame oil

1 tablespoon salt

1 teaspoon black pepper

2 tablespoons finely chopped garlic

2 tablespoons grated ginger

1 tablespoon shoyu

continued on the next page

1 tablespoon koo chu jung sauce
1 teaspoon sugar
1/2 cup chopped green onion
Man doo wrappers (oval/round)

Dipping Sauce:
3/4 cup shoyu
1/4 cup sugar
1/4 cup water
1/2 cup vinegar
2 tablespoons ground Korean chili pepper sauce
   (koo chu jung) or kim chee sauce
2 tablespoons finely chopped green onion
2 tablespoons finely chopped cilantro
1 tablespoon ground toasted sesame seeds
1 teaspoon grated ginger
1 teaspoon finely chopped garlic
1 tablespoon sesame seed oil

Finely chop the kim chee cabbage, tofu, and bean sprouts, and squeeze water out with a cheese cloth until dry. Add pork and rest of the ingredients and mix well.

Put a teaspoonful of mix onto a man doo wrapper and brush water on the edges. Fold in half to close into a half moon and crimp edges tight. Boil, deep-fry, or pan-fry for 4 minutes, or until done.

Mix all sauce ingredients together. Serve man doo with Dipping Sauce.

You can eat this traditionally with a homemade chicken broth that has been clarified and garnished with chopped scrambled egg, sliced nori, shredded chicken, sliced green onion, and a dash of toasted ground sesame seeds. You can also eat this as an appetizer without the broth, deep-fried or pan-fried, like gyoza. You can alter any of the ingredients to your personal taste. Enjoy!

Submitted by Chef and Owner Kelvin Ro,
Diamond Head Market and Grill

Mom Kodama's Brownie Recipe

Makes 24 to 48 brownies (depending upon how you cut it up)

This is Mom's original recipe. She developed it through the many years of cooking and baking for her family. Mom always did everything whole-heartedly and was ALWAYS full of life and grace. She actually trained all of our Sansei chefs to make her recipe. Having this recipe and sharing it with others is like having Mom back here in our kitchens.

1-1/2 cups unsalted butter, at room temperature
2 cups cocoa powder
4 cups sugar
8 eggs, lightly beaten
3 cups flour
2 teaspoons baking powder
2 teaspoons salt
2 cups chopped nuts, any kind
1 cup macadamia nuts, chopped

Preheat the oven to 350°F. Butter a 12 x 18-inch jelly roll pan or a baking sheet with sides.

In a saucepan, combine the butter and cocoa powder over medium heat, stir until melted and combined.

In a large bowl, combine the sugar and eggs. Add the cocoa mixture and mix gently. Into another bowl, sift the flour, baking powder, and salt, and add—a little at a time—to the wet ingredients, mixing until incorporated.

Fold in the nuts.

Pour the batter into the prepared pan and bake for 30 minutes, checking periodically, until a toothpick inserted in the center comes out clean. Let cool, then cut into bars or squares.

We do a Mom Kodama's Brownie Sundae by adding a scoop of vanilla ice cream topped with whipped cream, lots of chocolate sauce, and chopped macadamia nuts and a cherry.

Submitted by Ivy Nakagawa

Refrigerator Potato Rolls

Makes 3 dozen

Making refrigerator potato rolls was always memorable because of the aroma that only bread making can produce. The smell of the yeast while the rolls were rising in the bedroom, where it was nice and warm with the windows closed, then the aroma of the fresh rolls in the oven being baked, is just unforgettable! We made these for years, but one year we tried something new since Grandpa had a sweet tooth. This roll recipe evolved into anpan using tsubushian, a prepared sweetened azuki bean paste, which is stuffed into the rolls.

---

1 cup mashed potato
1/2 cup potato water, lukewarm
1 package active dry yeast
2/3 cup butter
2/3 cup sugar
2 teaspoons salt
1 cup milk, scalded
2 eggs, beaten
6 to 7 cups all-purpose flour, sifted
Butter for greasing and brushing

Peel, cube, and boil 1 large russet potato until soft. Reserve 1/2 cup potato water. Mash the potato and measure 1 cup.

Cool potato water to lukewarm and dissolve the yeast in it.

In a large mixing bowl combine the mashed potato, butter, sugar, salt, and hot milk. Cool. Stir in beaten eggs and dissolved yeast.

continued on the next page

Stir in flour with a wooden spoon and mix it until a soft dough develops. Gently knead and form the dough into a ball and place in a buttered bowl. Turn over to butter top, cover well, and refrigerate dough overnight.

Two hours before baking, remove dough from refrigerator and let temper about 1 hour. Then pinch walnut-size pieces off and roll into balls. Place on buttered baking pans 2 inches apart.

Cover with a dish cloth and place in a warm, draft-free area to proof and rise until double in size.

Bake in a 375 to 400°F preheated oven for 20 minutes until golden brown. Brush with butter if desired.

Option: To make anpan, flatten ball and add 1 tablespoon of prepared tsubushi-an into center of each dough roll and seal on bottom. Place on buttered pans and follow directions for rolls.

Submitted by Chef Mark Okumura

Glossary

A

'Ahi:
The Hawaiian name for both yellowfin and big eye tuna. Often served in the islands as sashimi (Japanese-style raw fish).

'Alae salt:
Traditional Hawaiian sea salt that is used for seasoning and preserving foods. Contains harvested reddish Hawaiian clay that adds iron-oxide.

B

Bean sprouts:
Fresh or canned sprouted mung beans.

C

Chinese cabbage (or won bok):
Pale green tops and white stems with crinkly leaves, also called napa cabbage or celery cabbage.

Chung choi
Salted turnip or radish.

Coconut milk:
A liquid extracted from shredded coconut meat.

D

Daikon:
Japanese name for a white, crisp radish. Turnips can be substituted.

Dried bean curd:
The skin of the tofu that has been dried.

G

Ginger:
A brown, fibrous, knobby rhizome that keeps for long periods of time. To use, peel the brown skin and slice, chop, or purée.

Guava:
A round tropical fruit with a yellow skin and pink inner flesh and many seeds. The purée or juice is available as a frozen concentrate. Guava can also be made into jams, jellies, and sauces.

H

Hawaiian chili pepper:
A very small (1/2 to 1-inch long) and extremely hot pepper, similar to the Caribbean bird chili.

Hawaiian salt:
A coarse sea salt gathered in tidal pools after a storm or high tide. Hawaiians sometimes mix it

with a red clay to make 'alae salt.
Substitute kosher salt.

J

Japanese rice vinegar:
A light vinegar made from fermented rice; generally clear with a pale straw color.

K

Kaong:
Sugar palm fruit.

Kim chee:
Korean hot, spicy, preserved vegetable, usually cabbage

Korean chili pepper sauce (or koo chu jung):
A spicy Korean bean paste sauce used for appetizers or flavorings.

L

Liliko'i:
The Hawaiian name for passionfruit, which is a small yellow, purple, or brown oval fruit of the passion fruit vine. The flavor is somewhat delicate but somewhat sharp, and perfume-like. Passion fruit is a natural substitute for lemon juice. Passion fruit concentrate can be found in the frozen juice section of many markets. Substitute oranges.

Liquid smoke:
Smoke that has been condensed into liquid form. Used for food preservation and flavoring.

Lomi salmon:
A fresh-tasting Hawaiian salad of salt-cured salmon, onion, and tomato.

Long rice:
A thin, clear noodle made from the starch of the mung bean. These relatively flavorless noodles soak up the flavors of other ingredients in the dish. They are also called cellophane or bean thread noodles.

Lū'au leaves:
The young, green tops of the taro root. Substitute fresh spinach.

M

Macapuno strings:
Made from macapuno nuts, which are anomolous coconuts.

Mahimahi:
Also called dolphinfish, with a firm, pink flesh. Best fresh, but often available frozen. A standard in island restaurants and markets. Substitute snapper, catfish, or halibut.

Macadamia nuts:
A rich, oily nut grown mostly on the Big Island of Hawai'i. Also called "mac nuts."

Mango:
Gold and green tropical fruit available fresh June through September in Hawai'i.

Maui onion:
A very sweet, juicy, large round onion similar to the Vidalia or Walla Walla onion. Often available on the West Coast, but expensive. Substitute any sweet white onion.

....

O

'Ōpakapaka:
A blue snapper with a delicate flavor. Good poached, baked, or sautéed. Substitute any red snapper, sea bass, or monkfish.

Oyster sauce:
A concentrated sauce made from oyster juice and salt, used in many Chinese and other Asian dishes. Keeps a long time in the refrigerator.

....

P

Pancit (or pansit):
Filipino noodles. Usually, refers to pancit bihon, which are a very thin rice noodles.

Parafin wax:
Food-grade parafin wax is used to seal jams and jellies in jars.

Pectin:
A food "glue" extracted from cit-rus fruits. Sold in powder or liquid forms.

Pineapple:
Fresh pineapples are covered with a prickly brown skin, and topped with sharp, pointed leaves. To select a fresh ripe pineapple, give the tiny center leaves at the top a light tug: The leaves will easily pluck out of ripe pineapple. Fresh pineapple contains an enzyme which will break down protein; rinse well and add as close to serving time as possible when using in dishes containing gelatin.

....

S

Sesame oil:
A strong-flavored oil made from toasted sesame seeds and used in most Asian cuisines. Only a small amount is needed for flavoring. Sesame oil burns at a lower heat than most oils. Refrigerate after opening.

Sesame seeds:
Small, flat, oval, white or black seeds used to flavor or garnish main dishes and desserts.

Shiitake mushrooms:
Medium to large with umbrella-shaped, flopped tan to dark brown caps with edges that tend to roll under. Shiitakes have a woodsy, smoky flavor. Can be purchased fresh or dried in Asian groceries. Dried shiitake need to be soaked in warm water until soft (20 to 30 minutes). Also called black Chinese mushrooms and golden oak mushrooms.

Shoyu (or soy sauce):
A dark, salty liquid made from
soybeans, flour, salt, and water.
Dark soy sauce is stronger than
light soy sauce. A staple in most
Asian cuisines.

....

T

Taro:
A starchy root of the taro, called
kalo. Its flavor is similar to arti-
chokes or chestnuts. The leaves
(lūʻau) and stems (hāhā) are also
used in cooking. Taro contains
an irritating substance and must
be cooked before any part of the
plant can be eaten.

Ti leaves:
Leaves of the ti plant, used to
steam and bake fish and vegetables. Often called "Hawaiian
aluminum foil." Substitute banana
leaves, grape leaves, or corn
husks. Available at wholesale flo-
ral shops.

Tofu:
Japanese name for a bland soy
bean curd that can be custard-
like in texture or quite firm. The
firm or extra firm varieties are
generally used in stir-frying or
deep-frying.